CURIOUS ABOUT ZOO VETS

by Gina Shaw

GROSSET & DUNLAP

An Imprint of Penguin Random House

GROSSET & DUNLAP

Penguin Young Readers Group
An Imprint of Penguin Random House LLC

 Smithsonian

This trademark is owned by the Smithsonian Institution and
is registered in the U.S. Patent and Trademark Office.

Smithsonian Enterprises:
Christopher Liedel, President
Carol LeBlanc, Senior Vice President, Education and Consumer Products
Brigid Ferraro, Vice President, Education and Consumer Products
Ellen Nanney, Licensing Manager
Kealy Gordon, Product Development Manager

Smithsonian's National Zoo:
Pamela Baker-Masson, Associate Director of Communications
Jen Zoon, Communications Specialist

PHOTO CREDITS: All photos © National Zoological Park, Smithsonian Institution;
photographers: Jessie Cohen, Connor Mallon, Meghan Murphy, Janice Sveda, Lisa Ware, Abby Wood.

Library of Congress Cataloging-in-Publication Data is available.

ISBN 978-0-448-48687-1   10 9 8 7 6 5 4 3 2 1

California sea lion

Who examines a young panda cub?

Or operates on a cheetah?

Or checks up on a sea lion with a bad tooth?

A ZOO VET does!

giant panda

A zoo **veterinarian** is a doctor who treats animals, not people. There are many veterinarians at Smithsonian's National Zoo in Washington, DC.

Veterinarians are also called vets. Most of them take care of pets like dogs, cats, and birds. But at the National Zoo, the vets treat wild animals like sloth bears, tigers, cheetahs, frogs, red pandas, kiwi, Komodo dragons, and many other animals.

cheetah

Zoo vets need to know everything about all kinds of animals, from head to tail! They are responsible for several thousand furry, feathered, prickly, slippery, or scaly animals at the National Zoo. These animals **represent** about three hundred different **species**.

siamang

red panda

toucan

emerald tree boa

white-naped crane

Aldabra tortoise

American bison

alpaca

North American porcupine

California sea lion

The Zoo's animals are divided into five different areas: mammals, birds, reptiles, amphibians, and fish. There is an animal leader for each area.

Every day is a busy day for the vets and the animal leaders. Each morning they all meet in the Zoo's hospital. Together, they decide which animals need medical attention. Then they write a schedule for the week.

Sumatran tiger

Next, they divide up their jobs for the day. Some vets, along with **veterinarian technicians**, work at the Zoo hospital. They will do wellness checkups on different animals. Each animal has a schedule for these **examinations**. This schedule is planned out for up to three years.

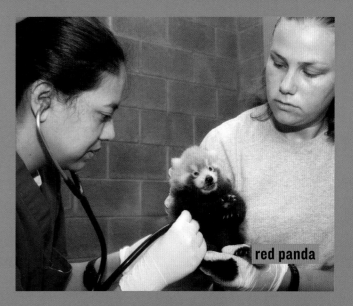
red panda

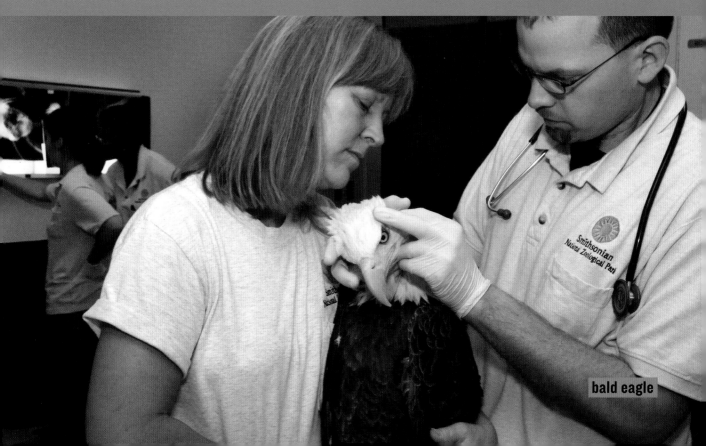
bald eagle

When the vets perform a wellness checkup, they listen to an animal's heart and lungs. They check its mouth, eyes, ears, legs, feet, and belly. They weigh it. They take its temperature. They give it shots. A vet's most important job is to keep every animal healthy and happy!

cheetah

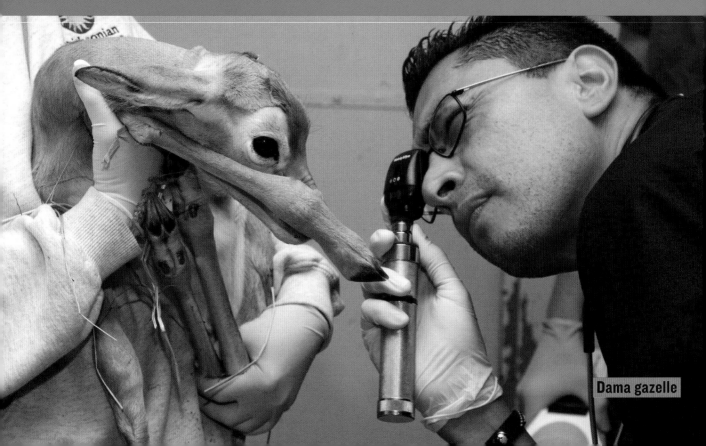

Dama gazelle

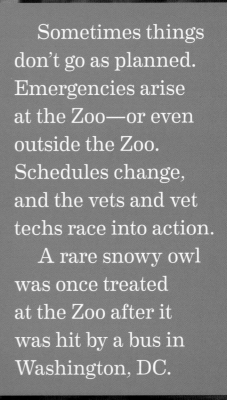

snowy owl

Sometimes things don't go as planned. Emergencies arise at the Zoo—or even outside the Zoo. Schedules change, and the vets and vet techs race into action.

A rare snowy owl was once treated at the Zoo after it was hit by a bus in Washington, DC.

While some Zoo vets work in the hospital, others examine the animals in their Zoo exhibits. Sometimes these animals have been injured, or they may be on **medication**. The vets want to be sure they're recovering.

When the vets visit the animals in their **enclosures**, the first thing they do is talk to the animal keepers. Keepers know the animals better than anyone else because they spend the most time with them. They are the first ones to notice any problems the animals might be having.

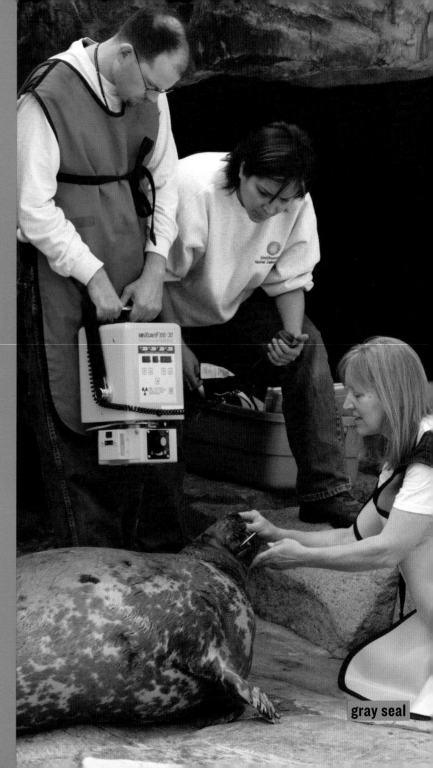

gray seal

At the National Zoo, the animal keepers take care of about 1,800 animals. What do these keepers do? Many, many things! Their days are very busy, and no two days are the same.

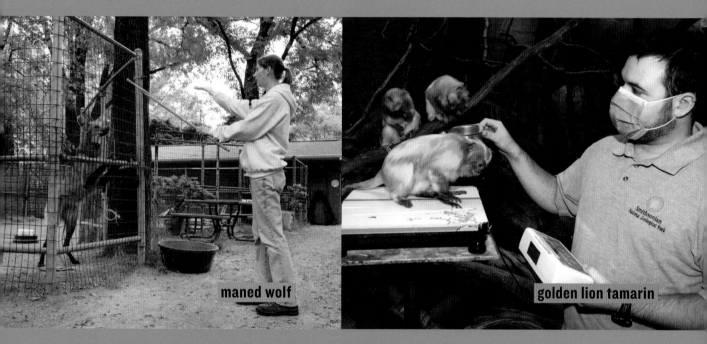

maned wolf

golden lion tamarin

One of their most important jobs is to interact with the animals. They are a team. Keepers work with the animals every day to gain their trust. They need to be able to trust the animals, too. This helps them provide the best care safely.

cheetah

Keepers watch the animals closely. They write a report about the animal's behavior every day. They want to make sure an animal is acting as it normally does. Is it eating enough? Is it sleeping too much? Is it limping? Did the animal stop playing or start acting strangely? If so, the keeper might call a vet to come and look at it.

Keepers take care of the Zoo animals' different needs every day, 365 days a year. They clip toenails, brush teeth, and give baths. They make sure the animals' areas are clean, safe, and well-supplied.

Asian elephant

Keepers also help with another very important job: feeding the animals!

western lowland gorilla

Some keepers work closely with the Zoo's **nutritionists** to prepare the best foods for every animal. In each exhibit's kitchen, keepers and **volunteers** chop carrots, slice apples, and open cans of food. They mix in medication if needed or prepare special treats. They do this every day, sometimes twice a day.

Next, other animal keepers bring the food to every enclosure. They feed the animals whatever has been specially prepared for them. Some animals even need to be fed around the clock—with a bottle!

kori bustard

American alligator

Keepers also train the animals. They teach them to open their mouths so the vets can get a good look inside. They train the animals so the vets can take their blood pressure. They help the animals learn to keep still during other exams.

African lion

iguana

Sometimes animals need to be moved to another part of the Zoo. The animal keepers show them how to enter and exit crates so they can be transported easily.

Training the animals makes it easier for Zoo vets and animal keepers to **monitor** their health and care for them.

The Zoo vets and animal keepers also want to make sure the animals are happy. The keepers create exhibit spaces that are similar to where animals would live in the wild. They encourage animals to make their own nests or homes in these areas. They want them to explore and behave like animals in the wild.

arapaima fish

black-footed ferret

Not long ago, there were only eighteen of these black-footed ferrets left in the wild in North America. The Zoo helps save **endangered** animals like this and returns some of them to the wild.

flamingo

golden lion tamarin

Everybody at the Zoo is happy when baby animals are born there. As the babies grow, they learn to live as if they were in the wild. This keeps them healthy and active. The Zoo also works with other **conservation centers** around the world to make sure enough different animal babies are born.

Asian elephant

cheetah

western lowland gorilla

red panda

scimitar-horned oryx

kiwi

Do the animals ever get bored? Not at the National Zoo! The animal keepers create **enrichment** activities for them. This could mean a tasty treat. Or a piece of cloth for snuggling. How about a ball to roll? Or something to hug?

western lowland gorilla

clouded leopard

Aldabra tortoise

African lion

ring-tailed lemur

One of the most popular forms of enrichment is food hide-and-seek! Animal keepers hide or scatter food in the Zoo enclosures. The animals hunt around for it as if they were in their natural **habitats**.

western lowland gorilla

Asian elephant

Asian small-clawed otter

Sometimes nature provides a great source of fun.

giant panda

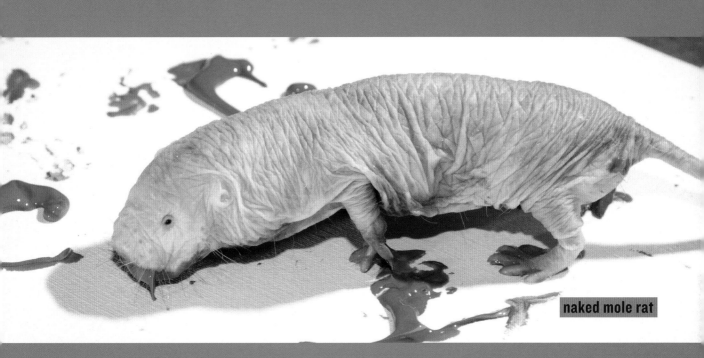

naked mole rat

So does art and even technology!

Bornean orangutan

Besides taking care of and training the animals, keepers also give **demonstrations** at the National Zoo throughout the day. They teach visitors about the animals. They talk about how important it is to **conserve** all animal species.

So many different animals.

So many different exhibits.

So many different jobs!

How about you?

Would you enjoy working at a Zoo?

GLOSSARY

conservation center: a place, like a Zoo, that works at protecting living things or natural spaces

conserve: to protect animals and plants from being harmed or wiped out entirely

demonstration: showing someone how something is used or done

enclosure: a space that is surrounded by something like a fence or a wall

endangered: a living thing that could die out and become extinct

enrichment: improving something by adding something to it

examination: a close and careful study of someone or something

habitat: the natural area where an animal or plant lives

medication: another word for medicine

monitor: to observe and keep track of something

nutritionist: a person who is trained to give advice on how foods affect people or animals' health

represent: to stand for something

species: a group of animals or plants that are similar and can produce young animals or plants

veterinarian: a doctor who is trained to give medical care and treatment to animals

veterinarian technician: a person who supports a veterinarian in all aspects of animal care except performing surgery, making a diagnosis, and prescribing medication

volunteer: a person who works or helps out but doesn't get paid